50 Vegetarian Thai Feast Recipes

By: Kelly Johnson

Table of Contents

- Pad Thai Jay (Vegetarian Pad Thai)
- Green Curry with Tofu (Gaeng Keow Wan Jay)
- Tom Yum Soup with Tofu (Tom Yum Tofu)
- Massaman Curry with Vegetables
- Red Curry with Eggplant (Gaeng Phed Makheua)
- Thai Basil Stir-Fried Tofu (Pad Krapow Tofu)
- Stir-Fried Vegetables with Cashews (Pad Pak Ruam Mit)
- Spicy Thai Noodle Salad (Yum Woon Sen Jay)
- Larb Tofu (Spicy Tofu Salad)
- Som Tum Jay (Vegetarian Green Papaya Salad)
- Thai Vegetable Spring Rolls
- Khao Pad Jay (Vegetarian Fried Rice)
- Vegetable Pad See Ew
- Tofu Satay with Peanut Sauce
- Thai Vegetable Soup (Tom Kha Jay)
- Thai Spicy Eggplant (Pad Makheua)
- Thai Mango Salad
- Thai Fried Tofu with Sweet Chili Sauce
- Thai Pumpkin Curry
- Thai Coconut Soup with Mushrooms
- Thai Cucumber Salad
- Thai Vegetable Curry (Gaeng Jay)
- Stir-Fried Thai Eggplant with Basil
- Thai Grilled Vegetable Skewers
- Thai Herb and Vegetable Salad
- Thai Corn Fritters
- Thai Sweet Potato and Coconut Soup
- Thai Rice Noodles with Peanut Sauce
- Thai Roasted Vegetable Salad
- Thai Tofu and Vegetable Hot Pot
- Thai Spicy Mango and Avocado Salad
- Thai Coconut Rice with Vegetables
- Thai Spicy Lentil Soup
- Thai Grilled Corn with Coconut Sauce
- Thai Stir-Fried Rice with Pineapple

- Thai Curry with Mixed Vegetables
- Thai Garlic Pepper Tofu
- Thai Cabbage Salad with Lime Dressing
- Thai Sweet Potato Curry
- Thai Noodle Soup with Tofu
- Thai Spinach Salad with Peanut Dressing
- Thai Mushroom and Tofu Stir-Fry
- Thai Green Bean Salad
- Thai Mixed Vegetable Curry
- Thai Tofu and Broccoli Stir-Fry
- Thai Pineapple Fried Rice
- Thai Red Lentil Curry
- Thai Chili Lime Quinoa Salad
- Thai Grilled Eggplant Salad
- Thai Stuffed Bell Peppers

Pad Thai Jay (Vegetarian Pad Thai)

Ingredients:

- 8 ounces rice noodles
- 1 tablespoon vegetable oil
- 2 cloves garlic, minced
- 1 cup firm tofu, cubed
- 1 cup bean sprouts
- 2 green onions, chopped
- 2 tablespoons soy sauce
- 1 tablespoon tamarind paste
- 1 tablespoon sugar
- Crushed peanuts, for garnish
- Lime wedges, for serving

Instructions:

1. **Prepare Noodles:**
    - Soak rice noodles in hot water until soft, then drain.
2. **Cook Tofu:**
    - In a large skillet, heat oil over medium heat. Add garlic and tofu, cooking until tofu is golden.
3. **Stir-Fry:**
    - Add soaked noodles, bean sprouts, green onions, soy sauce, tamarind paste, and sugar. Stir-fry for 3-5 minutes.
4. **Serve:**
    - Garnish with crushed peanuts and lime wedges before serving.

Green Curry with Tofu (Gaeng Keow Wan Jay)

Ingredients:

- 1 tablespoon vegetable oil
- 2-3 tablespoons green curry paste
- 1 can (400 ml) coconut milk
- 1 cup vegetable broth
- 1 cup firm tofu, cubed
- 1 cup mixed vegetables (bell peppers, zucchini, etc.)
- 2-3 kaffir lime leaves (optional)
- Fresh basil, for garnish

Instructions:

1. **Heat Oil:**
    - In a pot, heat oil over medium heat. Add green curry paste and cook until fragrant.
2. **Add Coconut Milk:**
    - Stir in coconut milk and vegetable broth. Bring to a simmer.
3. **Add Tofu and Vegetables:**
    - Add tofu, mixed vegetables, and kaffir lime leaves. Cook for 10-15 minutes until vegetables are tender.
4. **Serve:**
    - Garnish with fresh basil before serving.

Tom Yum Soup with Tofu (Tom Yum Tofu)

Ingredients:

- 4 cups vegetable broth
- 1 stalk lemongrass, chopped
- 3-4 kaffir lime leaves
- 2-3 slices galangal (or ginger)
- 1 cup mushrooms, sliced
- 1 cup firm tofu, cubed
- 2-3 tablespoons lime juice
- 2-3 tablespoons soy sauce
- Chili paste or fresh chilies, to taste
- Fresh cilantro, for garnish

Instructions:

1. **Prepare Broth:**
    - In a pot, bring vegetable broth to a boil. Add lemongrass, kaffir lime leaves, and galangal.
2. **Add Ingredients:**
    - Add mushrooms and tofu. Simmer for about 5-7 minutes.
3. **Season Soup:**
    - Stir in lime juice, soy sauce, and chili paste. Adjust seasoning to taste.
4. **Serve:**
    - Garnish with fresh cilantro before serving.

Massaman Curry with Vegetables

Ingredients:

- 1 tablespoon vegetable oil
- 2-3 tablespoons massaman curry paste
- 1 can (400 ml) coconut milk
- 1 cup vegetable broth
- 2 cups mixed vegetables (potatoes, carrots, etc.)
- 1 tablespoon soy sauce
- 1 tablespoon brown sugar
- Peanuts, for garnish

Instructions:

1. **Heat Oil:**
   - In a pot, heat oil over medium heat. Add massaman curry paste and cook until fragrant.
2. **Add Coconut Milk:**
   - Stir in coconut milk and vegetable broth. Bring to a simmer.
3. **Add Vegetables:**
   - Add mixed vegetables, soy sauce, and brown sugar. Cook until vegetables are tender.
4. **Serve:**
   - Garnish with peanuts before serving.

Red Curry with Eggplant (Gaeng Phed Makheua)

Ingredients:

- 1 tablespoon vegetable oil
- 2-3 tablespoons red curry paste
- 1 can (400 ml) coconut milk
- 1 cup vegetable broth
- 1-2 cups eggplant, cubed
- 1 cup mixed vegetables (bell peppers, broccoli, etc.)
- 2-3 tablespoons soy sauce
- Fresh basil, for garnish

Instructions:

1. **Heat Oil:**
    - In a pot, heat oil over medium heat. Add red curry paste and cook until fragrant.
2. **Add Coconut Milk:**
    - Stir in coconut milk and vegetable broth. Bring to a simmer.
3. **Add Vegetables:**
    - Add eggplant and mixed vegetables. Cook until tender. Stir in soy sauce.
4. **Serve:**
    - Garnish with fresh basil before serving.

Thai Basil Stir-Fried Tofu (Pad Krapow Tofu)

Ingredients:

- 1 tablespoon vegetable oil
- 2 cloves garlic, minced
- 1 cup firm tofu, crumbled
- 2-3 tablespoons soy sauce
- 1 tablespoon oyster sauce (or vegetarian substitute)
- 1-2 cups fresh basil leaves
- Cooked rice, for serving

Instructions:

1. **Heat Oil:**
    - In a skillet, heat oil over medium heat. Add garlic and sauté until fragrant.
2. **Add Tofu:**
    - Add crumbled tofu and cook until golden.
3. **Stir-Fry:**
    - Stir in soy sauce and oyster sauce. Add basil leaves and cook until wilted.
4. **Serve:**
    - Serve over cooked rice.

Stir-Fried Vegetables with Cashews (Pad Pak Ruam Mit)

Ingredients:

- 1 tablespoon vegetable oil
- 2 cloves garlic, minced
- 2 cups mixed vegetables (broccoli, bell peppers, carrots, etc.)
- 1/4 cup cashews
- 2-3 tablespoons soy sauce
- 1 tablespoon oyster sauce (or vegetarian substitute)

Instructions:

1. **Heat Oil:**
    - In a large skillet, heat oil over medium-high heat. Add garlic and sauté until fragrant.
2. **Add Vegetables:**
    - Add mixed vegetables and stir-fry for 3-4 minutes until tender-crisp.
3. **Add Cashews and Sauces:**
    - Stir in cashews, soy sauce, and oyster sauce. Cook for an additional 2-3 minutes.
4. **Serve:**
    - Serve hot.

Spicy Thai Noodle Salad (Yum Woon Sen Jay)

Ingredients:

- 8 ounces glass noodles
- 1 cup mixed vegetables (cucumber, carrots, bell peppers, etc.)
- 1/2 cup chopped cilantro
- 1/4 cup lime juice
- 2-3 tablespoons soy sauce
- 1 tablespoon chili paste
- Chopped peanuts, for garnish

Instructions:

1. **Prepare Noodles:**
   - Soak glass noodles in hot water until soft, then drain.
2. **Combine Ingredients:**
   - In a bowl, combine noodles, mixed vegetables, and cilantro.
3. **Make Dressing:**
   - In a separate bowl, whisk together lime juice, soy sauce, and chili paste.
4. **Toss Salad:**
   - Pour dressing over salad and toss to combine. Garnish with chopped peanuts before serving.

Larb Tofu (Spicy Tofu Salad)

Ingredients:

- 1 cup firm tofu, crumbled
- 2 tablespoons soy sauce
- 1 tablespoon lime juice
- 1 tablespoon roasted rice powder
- 1/2 red onion, thinly sliced
- 1 cup fresh herbs (mint, cilantro)
- 1-2 Thai chilies, chopped (optional)

Instructions:

1. **Cook Tofu:**
    - In a skillet, cook crumbled tofu over medium heat until golden. Remove from heat.
2. **Mix Ingredients:**
    - In a bowl, combine tofu, soy sauce, lime juice, roasted rice powder, red onion, herbs, and chilies.
3. **Serve:**
    - Serve chilled or at room temperature.

Som Tum Jay (Vegetarian Green Papaya Salad)

Ingredients:

- 2 cups shredded green papaya
- 1 carrot, shredded
- 1/2 cup cherry tomatoes, halved
- 2-3 tablespoons lime juice
- 2 tablespoons soy sauce
- 1 tablespoon palm sugar (or brown sugar)
- 1-2 Thai chilies, chopped (optional)
- Peanuts, for garnish

Instructions:

1. **Prepare Salad:**
   - In a large bowl, combine shredded papaya, carrot, and cherry tomatoes.
2. **Make Dressing:**
   - In a small bowl, whisk together lime juice, soy sauce, palm sugar, and chilies.
3. **Toss Salad:**
   - Pour dressing over salad and toss well. Garnish with peanuts before serving.

Thai Vegetable Spring Rolls

Ingredients:

- 8-10 rice paper wrappers
- 1 cup shredded vegetables (carrots, cucumbers, bell peppers)
- 1/2 cup fresh herbs (mint, cilantro)
- Lettuce leaves
- Dipping sauce (peanut sauce or sweet chili sauce)

Instructions:

1. **Prepare Wrappers:**
    - Soak rice paper wrappers in warm water until pliable.
2. **Fill Rolls:**
    - Place a lettuce leaf on the wrapper, add vegetables and herbs, then roll tightly.
3. **Serve:**
    - Serve with dipping sauce.

Khao Pad Jay (Vegetarian Fried Rice)

Ingredients:

- 2 cups cooked rice
- 2 tablespoons vegetable oil
- 2 cloves garlic, minced
- 1 cup mixed vegetables (peas, carrots, bell peppers)
- 2-3 tablespoons soy sauce
- 1 tablespoon lime juice
- Fresh cilantro, for garnish

Instructions:

1. **Heat Oil:**
    - In a skillet, heat oil over medium heat. Add garlic and sauté until fragrant.
2. **Add Vegetables:**
    - Stir in mixed vegetables and cook for 3-4 minutes.
3. **Add Rice:**
    - Add cooked rice, soy sauce, and lime juice. Stir-fry for another 3-4 minutes.
4. **Serve:**
    - Garnish with fresh cilantro before serving.

Vegetable Pad See Ew

Ingredients:

- 8 ounces wide rice noodles
- 2 tablespoons vegetable oil
- 2 cloves garlic, minced
- 1 cup mixed vegetables (broccoli, carrots, bell peppers)
- 2-3 tablespoons soy sauce
- 1 tablespoon dark soy sauce
- 1 tablespoon sugar

Instructions:

1. **Cook Noodles:**
   - Cook rice noodles according to package instructions; drain.
2. **Heat Oil:**
   - In a large skillet, heat oil over medium-high heat. Add garlic and sauté.
3. **Add Vegetables:**
   - Stir in mixed vegetables and cook until tender.
4. **Add Noodles and Sauces:**
   - Add cooked noodles, soy sauce, dark soy sauce, and sugar. Toss well to combine.
5. **Serve:**
   - Serve hot.

Tofu Satay with Peanut Sauce

Ingredients:

- 1 block firm tofu, pressed and cut into strips
- 1 tablespoon soy sauce
- 1 tablespoon curry powder
- 1 tablespoon vegetable oil
- Peanut sauce (store-bought or homemade)

Instructions:

1. **Marinate Tofu:**
    - In a bowl, combine tofu, soy sauce, curry powder, and oil. Let marinate for at least 30 minutes.
2. **Grill Tofu:**
    - Preheat grill or skillet over medium heat. Grill tofu strips until golden.
3. **Serve:**
    - Serve with peanut sauce for dipping.

Thai Vegetable Soup (Tom Kha Jay)

Ingredients:

- 4 cups vegetable broth
- 1 stalk lemongrass, chopped
- 3-4 kaffir lime leaves
- 1 cup mushrooms, sliced
- 1 cup mixed vegetables (carrots, bell peppers)
- 1 can (400 ml) coconut milk
- 2-3 tablespoons lime juice
- Fresh cilantro, for garnish

Instructions:

1. **Prepare Broth:**
    - In a pot, bring vegetable broth to a boil. Add lemongrass and kaffir lime leaves.
2. **Add Vegetables:**
    - Stir in mushrooms and mixed vegetables. Cook for about 5-7 minutes.
3. **Add Coconut Milk:**
    - Pour in coconut milk and simmer for 2-3 minutes.
4. **Serve:**
    - Stir in lime juice and garnish with fresh cilantro before serving.

Thai Spicy Eggplant (Pad Makheua)

Ingredients:

- 2 cups eggplant, sliced
- 2 tablespoons vegetable oil
- 2 cloves garlic, minced
- 2-3 tablespoons soy sauce
- 1 tablespoon chili paste
- Fresh basil, for garnish

Instructions:

1. **Heat Oil:**
    - In a skillet, heat oil over medium heat. Add garlic and sauté until fragrant.
2. **Add Eggplant:**
    - Stir in sliced eggplant and cook until tender.
3. **Add Sauces:**
    - Stir in soy sauce and chili paste. Cook for another 2-3 minutes.
4. **Serve:**
    - Garnish with fresh basil before serving.

Thai Mango Salad

Ingredients:

- 2 ripe mangoes, julienned
- 1 carrot, julienned
- 1/2 red onion, thinly sliced
- 1/4 cup fresh cilantro, chopped
- 2 tablespoons lime juice
- 1 tablespoon fish sauce (or soy sauce for a vegetarian version)
- 1 tablespoon sugar
- 1-2 Thai chilies, chopped (optional)

Instructions:

1. **Prepare Salad:**
   - In a large bowl, combine mangoes, carrot, red onion, and cilantro.
2. **Make Dressing:**
   - In a small bowl, whisk together lime juice, fish sauce, sugar, and chilies.
3. **Toss Salad:**
   - Pour dressing over salad and toss well before serving.

Thai Fried Tofu with Sweet Chili Sauce

Ingredients:

- 1 block firm tofu, cubed
- 1/2 cup cornstarch
- Oil for frying
- Sweet chili sauce for dipping

Instructions:

1. **Coat Tofu:**
    - Toss tofu cubes in cornstarch until evenly coated.
2. **Fry Tofu:**
    - Heat oil in a frying pan over medium heat. Fry tofu until golden and crispy on all sides.
3. **Serve:**
    - Serve hot with sweet chili sauce.

Thai Pumpkin Curry

Ingredients:

- 2 cups pumpkin, diced
- 1 can (400 ml) coconut milk
- 2 tablespoons red curry paste
- 1 tablespoon soy sauce
- 1 cup vegetable broth
- Fresh basil for garnish

Instructions:

1. **Cook Pumpkin:**
   - In a pot, combine pumpkin, coconut milk, curry paste, soy sauce, and vegetable broth. Bring to a boil.
2. **Simmer:**
   - Reduce heat and simmer until pumpkin is tender, about 15-20 minutes.
3. **Serve:**
   - Garnish with fresh basil before serving.

Thai Coconut Soup with Mushrooms

Ingredients:

- 4 cups vegetable broth
- 1 can (400 ml) coconut milk
- 1 cup mushrooms, sliced
- 2-3 kaffir lime leaves
- 1 stalk lemongrass, chopped
- 2-3 tablespoons lime juice

Instructions:

1. **Prepare Broth:**
    - In a pot, bring vegetable broth to a boil. Add coconut milk, mushrooms, lime leaves, and lemongrass.
2. **Simmer:**
    - Cook for about 10 minutes until mushrooms are tender.
3. **Serve:**
    - Stir in lime juice before serving.

Thai Cucumber Salad

Ingredients:

- 2 cucumbers, thinly sliced
- 1/2 red onion, thinly sliced
- 1/4 cup fresh cilantro, chopped
- 2 tablespoons vinegar
- 1 tablespoon sugar
- Salt to taste

Instructions:

1. **Combine Ingredients:**
    - In a bowl, mix cucumbers, red onion, and cilantro.
2. **Make Dressing:**
    - In a separate bowl, whisk together vinegar, sugar, and salt.
3. **Toss Salad:**
    - Pour dressing over the salad and toss well before serving.

Thai Vegetable Curry (Gaeng Jay)

Ingredients:

- 2 cups mixed vegetables (carrots, bell peppers, zucchini)
- 1 can (400 ml) coconut milk
- 2 tablespoons red curry paste
- 1 tablespoon soy sauce
- Fresh basil for garnish

Instructions:

1. **Cook Vegetables:**
    - In a pot, combine mixed vegetables, coconut milk, curry paste, and soy sauce. Bring to a boil.
2. **Simmer:**
    - Reduce heat and simmer until vegetables are tender, about 10-15 minutes.
3. **Serve:**
    - Garnish with fresh basil before serving.

Stir-Fried Thai Eggplant with Basil

Ingredients:

- 2 cups Thai eggplant, sliced
- 2 tablespoons vegetable oil
- 2 cloves garlic, minced
- 2-3 tablespoons soy sauce
- Fresh basil leaves

Instructions:

1. **Heat Oil:**
    - In a skillet, heat oil over medium heat. Add garlic and sauté until fragrant.
2. **Add Eggplant:**
    - Stir in eggplant slices and cook until tender.
3. **Add Sauces:**
    - Add soy sauce and basil. Stir-fry for another 2-3 minutes.
4. **Serve:**
    - Serve hot.

Thai Grilled Vegetable Skewers

Ingredients:

- 2 cups mixed vegetables (bell peppers, zucchini, mushrooms)
- 2 tablespoons vegetable oil
- 2 tablespoons soy sauce
- 1 tablespoon honey (or maple syrup)

Instructions:

1. **Prepare Marinade:**
   - In a bowl, mix oil, soy sauce, and honey.
2. **Marinate Vegetables:**
   - Toss vegetables in the marinade and let sit for 30 minutes.
3. **Grill Skewers:**
   - Thread vegetables onto skewers and grill until tender, about 10-15 minutes.
4. **Serve:**
   - Serve warm.

Thai Herb and Vegetable Salad

Ingredients:

- 2 cups mixed salad greens
- 1 cup cherry tomatoes, halved
- 1/2 cucumber, sliced
- 1/4 cup fresh herbs (mint, cilantro, basil)
- 2 tablespoons lime juice
- 1 tablespoon fish sauce (or soy sauce for a vegetarian version)

Instructions:

1. **Prepare Salad:**
   - In a large bowl, combine salad greens, tomatoes, cucumber, and herbs.
2. **Make Dressing:**
   - In a small bowl, whisk together lime juice and fish sauce.
3. **Toss Salad:**
   - Pour dressing over the salad and toss well before serving.

Thai Corn Fritters

Ingredients:

- 1 cup corn kernels (fresh or canned)
- 1/2 cup rice flour
- 1/4 cup all-purpose flour
- 1/4 cup coconut milk
- 1 egg, beaten
- 1/4 cup green onions, chopped
- Oil for frying
- Salt and pepper to taste

Instructions:

1. **Prepare Batter:**
    - In a bowl, combine corn, rice flour, all-purpose flour, coconut milk, beaten egg, green onions, salt, and pepper.
2. **Heat Oil:**
    - In a frying pan, heat oil over medium heat.
3. **Fry Fritters:**
    - Drop spoonfuls of the batter into the hot oil and fry until golden brown on both sides.
4. **Serve:**
    - Drain on paper towels and serve warm.

Thai Sweet Potato and Coconut Soup

Ingredients:

- 2 cups sweet potatoes, peeled and diced
- 1 can (400 ml) coconut milk
- 4 cups vegetable broth
- 1 onion, chopped
- 2 cloves garlic, minced
- 1 tablespoon ginger, grated
- Salt and pepper to taste

Instructions:

1. **Cook Onions:**
   - In a pot, sauté onion, garlic, and ginger until fragrant.
2. **Add Sweet Potatoes:**
   - Add sweet potatoes and vegetable broth. Bring to a boil.
3. **Simmer:**
   - Reduce heat and simmer until sweet potatoes are tender, about 15-20 minutes.
4. **Blend Soup:**
   - Stir in coconut milk, then blend until smooth. Season with salt and pepper before serving.

Thai Rice Noodles with Peanut Sauce

Ingredients:

- 8 oz rice noodles
- 1/2 cup peanut butter
- 2 tablespoons soy sauce
- 1 tablespoon lime juice
- 1 tablespoon honey
- 1 clove garlic, minced
- Chopped peanuts and cilantro for garnish

Instructions:

1. **Cook Noodles:**
    - Cook rice noodles according to package instructions. Drain and set aside.
2. **Make Sauce:**
    - In a bowl, whisk together peanut butter, soy sauce, lime juice, honey, and garlic.
3. **Combine:**
    - Toss cooked noodles with peanut sauce until well coated.
4. **Serve:**
    - Garnish with chopped peanuts and cilantro before serving.

Thai Roasted Vegetable Salad

Ingredients:

- 2 cups mixed vegetables (bell peppers, zucchini, carrots)
- 2 tablespoons olive oil
- Salt and pepper to taste
- 2 cups mixed salad greens
- 2 tablespoons lime juice
- Fresh herbs for garnish

Instructions:

1. **Roast Vegetables:**
    - Preheat oven to 400°F (200°C). Toss vegetables with olive oil, salt, and pepper. Spread on a baking sheet and roast for 20-25 minutes.
2. **Combine Salad:**
    - In a bowl, combine roasted vegetables with salad greens.
3. **Dress Salad:**
    - Drizzle with lime juice and toss gently.
4. **Serve:**
    - Garnish with fresh herbs before serving.

Thai Tofu and Vegetable Hot Pot

Ingredients:

- 1 block firm tofu, cubed
- 2 cups mixed vegetables (broccoli, bell peppers, carrots)
- 4 cups vegetable broth
- 1 tablespoon soy sauce
- 1 tablespoon sesame oil
- Fresh cilantro for garnish

Instructions:

1. **Heat Broth:**
   - In a pot, bring vegetable broth to a simmer. Add soy sauce and sesame oil.
2. **Add Tofu and Vegetables:**
   - Add cubed tofu and mixed vegetables to the pot. Cook until vegetables are tender.
3. **Serve:**
   - Garnish with fresh cilantro before serving.

Thai Spicy Mango and Avocado Salad

Ingredients:

- 1 ripe mango, diced
- 1 avocado, diced
- 1/2 red onion, thinly sliced
- 1 tablespoon lime juice
- 1-2 Thai chilies, chopped (optional)
- Salt to taste
- Fresh cilantro for garnish

Instructions:

1. **Combine Ingredients:**
    - In a bowl, combine mango, avocado, red onion, lime juice, chilies, and salt.
2. **Toss Gently:**
    - Toss gently to combine, being careful not to mash the avocado.
3. **Serve:**
    - Garnish with fresh cilantro before serving.

Thai Coconut Rice with Vegetables

Ingredients:

- 1 cup jasmine rice
- 1 can (400 ml) coconut milk
- 1 cup vegetable broth
- 1 cup mixed vegetables (peas, carrots, bell peppers)
- Salt to taste

Instructions:

1. **Cook Rice:**
     - Rinse rice under cold water. In a pot, combine rice, coconut milk, vegetable broth, and salt. Bring to a boil.
2. **Simmer:**
     - Reduce heat, cover, and simmer until rice is tender and liquid is absorbed, about 15-20 minutes.
3. **Add Vegetables:**
     - Stir in mixed vegetables and let sit for 5 minutes before serving.

Thai Spicy Lentil Soup

Ingredients:

- 1 cup lentils, rinsed
- 4 cups vegetable broth
- 1 onion, chopped
- 2 cloves garlic, minced
- 1 tablespoon red curry paste
- 1 can (400 ml) coconut milk
- Salt and pepper to taste

Instructions:

1. **Cook Onions:**
    - In a pot, sauté onion and garlic until fragrant. Add red curry paste and stir for 1 minute.
2. **Add Lentils and Broth:**
    - Add lentils and vegetable broth. Bring to a boil, then reduce heat and simmer until lentils are tender, about 20-25 minutes.
3. **Blend Soup:**
    - Stir in coconut milk and season with salt and pepper before serving.

Thai Grilled Corn with Coconut Sauce

Ingredients:

- 4 ears of corn, husked
- 1 can (400 ml) coconut milk
- 2 tablespoons sugar
- 1 teaspoon salt
- Fresh cilantro for garnish

Instructions:

1. **Grill Corn:**
    - Preheat grill to medium-high. Grill corn, turning occasionally, until charred and cooked, about 10-15 minutes.
2. **Make Coconut Sauce:**
    - In a saucepan, combine coconut milk, sugar, and salt. Heat gently until sugar dissolves.
3. **Serve:**
    - Brush grilled corn with coconut sauce and garnish with cilantro.

Thai Stir-Fried Rice with Pineapple

Ingredients:

- 2 cups cooked jasmine rice
- 1 cup pineapple chunks
- 1 cup mixed vegetables (carrots, peas, bell peppers)
- 2 tablespoons soy sauce
- 1 tablespoon vegetable oil
- 2 eggs, beaten
- Green onions for garnish

Instructions:

1. **Heat Oil:**
    - In a large skillet or wok, heat vegetable oil over medium heat.
2. **Scramble Eggs:**
    - Add beaten eggs and scramble until cooked. Remove and set aside.
3. **Stir-Fry Vegetables:**
    - In the same pan, add mixed vegetables and pineapple. Stir-fry for 3-4 minutes.
4. **Combine:**
    - Add cooked rice and soy sauce, stirring to combine. Return scrambled eggs to the pan and mix well.
5. **Serve:**
    - Garnish with chopped green onions before serving.

Thai Curry with Mixed Vegetables

Ingredients:

- 1 tablespoon red curry paste
- 1 can (400 ml) coconut milk
- 2 cups mixed vegetables (bell peppers, broccoli, carrots)
- 1 tablespoon soy sauce
- 1 tablespoon vegetable oil
- Fresh basil for garnish

Instructions:

1. **Heat Oil:**
   - In a pot, heat vegetable oil over medium heat. Add red curry paste and sauté for 1-2 minutes.
2. **Add Coconut Milk:**
   - Stir in coconut milk and bring to a simmer.
3. **Add Vegetables:**
   - Add mixed vegetables and soy sauce. Cook until vegetables are tender, about 10 minutes.
4. **Serve:**
   - Garnish with fresh basil before serving.

Thai Garlic Pepper Tofu

Ingredients:

- 1 block firm tofu, cubed
- 4 cloves garlic, minced
- 2 tablespoons soy sauce
- 1 tablespoon black pepper
- 2 tablespoons vegetable oil
- Chopped cilantro for garnish

Instructions:

1. **Cook Tofu:**
    - In a skillet, heat vegetable oil over medium-high heat. Add cubed tofu and cook until golden brown.
2. **Add Garlic:**
    - Add minced garlic and cook for an additional minute.
3. **Season:**
    - Stir in soy sauce and black pepper, mixing well.
4. **Serve:**
    - Garnish with chopped cilantro before serving.

Thai Cabbage Salad with Lime Dressing

Ingredients:

- 4 cups cabbage, shredded
- 1 carrot, grated
- 1/4 cup fresh cilantro, chopped
- 1/4 cup lime juice
- 2 tablespoons sugar
- Salt and pepper to taste

Instructions:

1. **Make Dressing:**
   - In a bowl, whisk together lime juice, sugar, salt, and pepper until sugar dissolves.
2. **Combine Salad:**
   - In a large bowl, combine cabbage, carrot, and cilantro.
3. **Dress Salad:**
   - Pour dressing over the salad and toss to combine.
4. **Serve:**
   - Let sit for a few minutes before serving to allow flavors to meld.

Thai Sweet Potato Curry

Ingredients:

- 2 cups sweet potatoes, peeled and diced
- 1 can (400 ml) coconut milk
- 1 tablespoon red curry paste
- 1 cup vegetable broth
- 1 tablespoon vegetable oil
- Fresh basil for garnish

Instructions:

1. **Heat Oil:**
    - In a pot, heat vegetable oil over medium heat. Add red curry paste and sauté for 1-2 minutes.
2. **Add Sweet Potatoes:**
    - Stir in sweet potatoes, coconut milk, and vegetable broth. Bring to a simmer.
3. **Cook:**
    - Cook until sweet potatoes are tender, about 15-20 minutes.
4. **Serve:**
    - Garnish with fresh basil before serving.

Thai Noodle Soup with Tofu

Ingredients:

- 8 oz rice noodles
- 4 cups vegetable broth
- 1 block firm tofu, cubed
- 2 cups mixed vegetables (bok choy, mushrooms, carrots)
- 2 tablespoons soy sauce
- 1 tablespoon lime juice
- Fresh cilantro for garnish

Instructions:

1. **Cook Noodles:**
    - Cook rice noodles according to package instructions. Drain and set aside.
2. **Heat Broth:**
    - In a pot, bring vegetable broth to a simmer. Add cubed tofu and mixed vegetables.
3. **Season:**
    - Stir in soy sauce and lime juice. Simmer until vegetables are tender.
4. **Serve:**
    - Serve soup over cooked noodles and garnish with fresh cilantro.

Thai Spinach Salad with Peanut Dressing

Ingredients:

- 4 cups fresh spinach
- 1/2 cup cucumber, sliced
- 1/4 cup red bell pepper, sliced
- 1/4 cup roasted peanuts, chopped
- 1/4 cup peanut butter
- 2 tablespoons soy sauce
- 1 tablespoon lime juice
- 1 tablespoon honey

Instructions:

1. **Make Dressing:**
   - In a bowl, whisk together peanut butter, soy sauce, lime juice, and honey until smooth.
2. **Combine Salad:**
   - In a large bowl, combine spinach, cucumber, red bell pepper, and chopped peanuts.
3. **Dress Salad:**
   - Pour peanut dressing over the salad and toss to coat.
4. **Serve:**
   - Serve immediately for the freshest taste.

Thai Mushroom and Tofu Stir-Fry

Ingredients:

- 1 block firm tofu, cubed
- 2 cups mushrooms, sliced
- 1 bell pepper, sliced
- 2 cloves garlic, minced
- 2 tablespoons soy sauce
- 1 tablespoon vegetable oil
- 1 tablespoon cornstarch
- Green onions for garnish

Instructions:

1. **Prepare Tofu:**
   - Toss cubed tofu with cornstarch. In a skillet, heat vegetable oil over medium-high heat.
2. **Cook Tofu:**
   - Add tofu and cook until golden on all sides. Remove and set aside.
3. **Stir-Fry Vegetables:**
   - In the same skillet, add garlic, mushrooms, and bell pepper. Stir-fry for 4-5 minutes.
4. **Combine:**
   - Return tofu to the pan, add soy sauce, and mix well.
5. **Serve:**
   - Garnish with sliced green onions before serving.

Thai Green Bean Salad

Ingredients:

- 2 cups green beans, trimmed and blanched
- 1 cup cherry tomatoes, halved
- 1/4 cup red onion, thinly sliced
- 1/4 cup fresh cilantro, chopped
- 2 tablespoons lime juice
- 1 tablespoon fish sauce (or soy sauce for vegetarian)
- 1 teaspoon sugar

Instructions:

1. **Make Dressing:**
   - In a small bowl, whisk together lime juice, fish sauce, and sugar until dissolved.
2. **Combine Salad:**
   - In a large bowl, combine blanched green beans, cherry tomatoes, red onion, and cilantro.
3. **Dress Salad:**
   - Pour dressing over the salad and toss to combine.
4. **Serve:**
   - Serve immediately or chill for a bit before serving.

Thai Mixed Vegetable Curry

Ingredients:

- 1 can (400 ml) coconut milk
- 2 tablespoons red curry paste
- 2 cups mixed vegetables (carrots, bell peppers, zucchini)
- 1 tablespoon soy sauce
- 1 tablespoon vegetable oil
- Fresh basil for garnish

Instructions:

1. **Heat Oil:**
   - In a pot, heat vegetable oil over medium heat. Add red curry paste and sauté for 1-2 minutes.
2. **Add Coconut Milk:**
   - Stir in coconut milk and bring to a simmer.
3. **Add Vegetables:**
   - Add mixed vegetables and soy sauce. Cook until vegetables are tender, about 10 minutes.
4. **Serve:**
   - Garnish with fresh basil before serving.

Thai Tofu and Broccoli Stir-Fry

Ingredients:

- 1 block firm tofu, cubed
- 2 cups broccoli florets
- 1 bell pepper, sliced
- 2 cloves garlic, minced
- 2 tablespoons soy sauce
- 1 tablespoon vegetable oil
- 1 teaspoon sesame oil

Instructions:

1. **Cook Tofu:**
    - In a skillet, heat vegetable oil over medium-high heat. Add cubed tofu and cook until golden brown. Remove and set aside.
2. **Stir-Fry Vegetables:**
    - In the same skillet, add garlic, broccoli, and bell pepper. Stir-fry for 4-5 minutes.
3. **Combine:**
    - Return tofu to the pan, add soy sauce and sesame oil, and mix well.
4. **Serve:**
    - Serve hot with rice.

Thai Pineapple Fried Rice

Ingredients:

- 2 cups cooked jasmine rice
- 1 cup pineapple chunks
- 1/2 cup peas and carrots
- 2 green onions, sliced
- 2 tablespoons soy sauce
- 1 tablespoon curry powder
- 1 tablespoon vegetable oil

Instructions:

1. **Heat Oil:**
    - In a large skillet, heat vegetable oil over medium heat. Add cooked rice and stir-fry for 2-3 minutes.
2. **Add Vegetables:**
    - Stir in pineapple, peas, carrots, and curry powder. Cook for an additional 3-4 minutes.
3. **Season:**
    - Add soy sauce and sliced green onions. Stir to combine.
4. **Serve:**
    - Serve warm as a main or side dish.

Thai Red Lentil Curry

Ingredients:

- 1 cup red lentils, rinsed
- 1 can (400 ml) coconut milk
- 2 cups vegetable broth
- 2 tablespoons red curry paste
- 1 tablespoon vegetable oil
- Fresh cilantro for garnish

Instructions:

1. **Heat Oil:**
   - In a pot, heat vegetable oil over medium heat. Add red curry paste and sauté for 1-2 minutes.
2. **Add Lentils:**
   - Stir in lentils, coconut milk, and vegetable broth. Bring to a simmer.
3. **Cook:**
   - Cook until lentils are tender, about 20 minutes.
4. **Serve:**
   - Garnish with fresh cilantro before serving.

Thai Chili Lime Quinoa Salad

Ingredients:

- 1 cup quinoa, cooked
- 1 cup cherry tomatoes, halved
- 1/2 cucumber, diced
- 1/4 cup red onion, diced
- 1/4 cup lime juice
- 1 tablespoon fish sauce (or soy sauce for vegetarian)
- 1 teaspoon chili flakes
- Fresh cilantro for garnish

Instructions:

1. **Make Dressing:**
    - In a small bowl, whisk together lime juice, fish sauce, and chili flakes.
2. **Combine Salad:**
    - In a large bowl, combine cooked quinoa, cherry tomatoes, cucumber, and red onion.
3. **Dress Salad:**
    - Pour dressing over the salad and toss to combine.
4. **Serve:**
    - Garnish with fresh cilantro before serving.

Thai Grilled Eggplant Salad

Ingredients:

- 2 eggplants, sliced
- 1/4 cup fish sauce (or soy sauce for vegetarian)
- 2 tablespoons lime juice
- 1 tablespoon sugar
- 2 cloves garlic, minced
- Fresh basil for garnish

Instructions:

1. **Grill Eggplant:**
    - Preheat grill. Grill eggplant slices until tender and charred, about 5-7 minutes per side.
2. **Make Dressing:**
    - In a bowl, whisk together fish sauce, lime juice, sugar, and garlic.
3. **Combine:**
    - In a serving dish, arrange grilled eggplant and drizzle with dressing.
4. **Serve:**
    - Garnish with fresh basil before serving.

Thai Stuffed Bell Peppers

Ingredients:

- 4 bell peppers, halved and seeded
- 1 cup cooked quinoa or rice
- 1 cup mixed vegetables (corn, peas, carrots)
- 1/4 cup soy sauce
- 1 tablespoon curry powder
- 1 tablespoon vegetable oil

Instructions:

1. **Preheat Oven:**
    - Preheat oven to 375°F (190°C).
2. **Prepare Filling:**
    - In a bowl, combine cooked quinoa or rice, mixed vegetables, soy sauce, and curry powder.
3. **Stuff Peppers:**
    - Stuff each bell pepper half with the filling.
4. **Bake:**
    - Place stuffed peppers in a baking dish and bake for 25-30 minutes until peppers are tender.
5. **Serve:**
    - Serve warm as a main or side dish.

www.ingramcontent.com/pod-product-compliance
Lightning Source LLC
LaVergne TN
LVHW081507060526
838201LV00056BA/2977